something flown

something flown

Patty Crane

Concrete Wolf
Poetry Chapbook
Award Series

Copyright © 2018 Patty Crane

All rights reserved. No part of this publication may be reproduced, distributed, or transmitted in any form, or by any means whatsoever, without written permission from the publisher, except in the case of brief excerpts for critical reviews and articles. All inquiries should be addressed to MoonPath Press.

Poetry
ISBN 978-0-9964754-8-8

Design: Tonya Namura using
New Cicle (display) and Liberation Sans (text)

Cover art: "Moonbird I: Tierra del Fuego"
collagraph monoprint
by artist Kate Cheney Chappell

Author photo: Eric Korenman

Concrete Wolf Poetry Chapbook Award Series
Concrete Wolf
PO Box 445
Tillamook, OR 97141

http://ConcreteWolf.com

ConcreteWolfPress@gmail.com

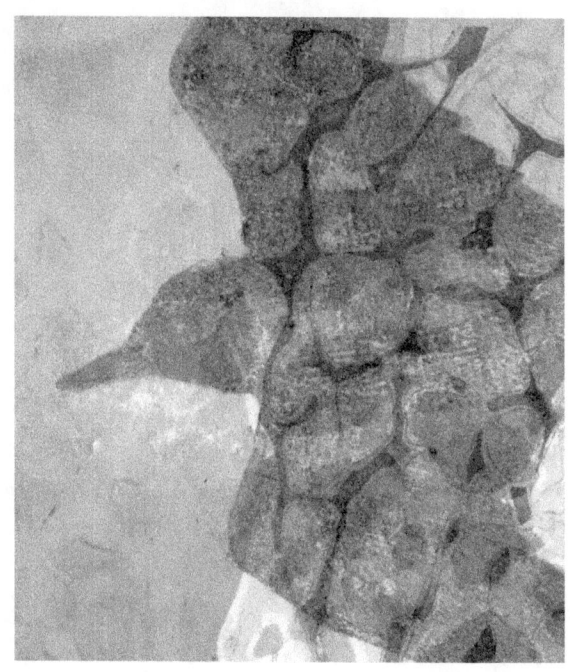

For do you not see how everything that happens keeps on being a beginning...?
—Rilke

Contents

i.

The birds this morning	5
Here	6
In the beginning	7
again	8
if X = bird	9
this sense	10
The project	11

ii.

In the beginning	15
A city mortar-ripped	17
snow	18
Bird is	19
the thicket	20
breathe	21
flock	22
Why bird	23
my cage	24

iii.

my desk	27
two grouse	28
Dusk	29
lost again	30
Nothing wants to be itself	31
fox	33
Cold the day	34

Acknowledgments	37
About the Author	39

something
flown

i.

                The birds this morning are full-
           feathered   lofted to buffer the cold
                   now five below
                                        and dropping
            There's a peace
              to their endless back and forth
                                 their desperation
                  and it flickers
                  in my side-vision:
                                     bird here then gone
                                          then here again

                    and I call them
                 nuthatch   chickadee   jay
            until name becomes loss
            and loss becomes flight
                          and I am   tongue-tied
                                         wing-tied

                              *

                    Form is the shape of the vessel
                              Formlessness: form
                                               set free

                              One goes
                                where one is called

Here is a thing I cannot grasp
        Shape of the vessel
           is flight: is here then gone
                              then here again

    One bird takes off   another lands

    Permanence has left   transience
      is back   and they gather
                    gather and fill

 In winter they can't stop
or else they'll cease   Each seed
              a log on the fire of life
Shape of the vessel is smoke

                    In the beginning
                            God

        (why God
                    why not   bird)

                    In the beginning
                            bird
                    created heaven and earth
                    and earth was without form
                                and void   and darkness
                            was on the face of the deep

            then a spirit moved
        the heavens opened and
                                            Let there be flight

                    This can't be right

       It's snowing   again:
            birds at the feeder   here then gone
                                                        then here   again
                Snow is a blink
          bird is a blink   and the spider balled up
      under the peeling bark of a birch
               is a blink

            Blink   and you are gone
      Blink   and you go blind
           back to the original dark:
without form and void
                  before you open your eyes
and look what's holding the world
          on its tiny feathered back

    Look at the feeder
                  full of their flickering
   And they can't stop
         or else they'll cease
holding the world up

if X = bird

      X took xself off the map
               upped and went like a god
taking all it owned
          which was nothing much—
a gullet-full—   and just flew

And we bewitch ourselves
            with X's absence
  our longing   our grief

                                           This can't
                                           be right

There is this sense
            of being here
    not long
        not knowing if there
    is any sense

    just this   snow
            catching in the larch
                this sky
    always
            never the same

There is the we of us
    which is a myth
            and the I (the X)   which is flight

trust trust the season speaks
   who is everything
            round and coming back
                    full of its own vanishing

    The project   is to look
                      at the bird
  not there anymore:
                  the after-bird

     If only I could see
              straight
              but everything's moving:

these snowfields   the mountain
      that hatchwork of trees
            linked by
bird after bird after bird

                            the feeder still swinging
                    from the sudden weight
                              of the last one leaving

               *

    You flickering vessel
my love my pest   Come find me

         I am the horizon

ii.

                    In the beginning
        was a glitch:
                        God or no god   (bird or no)
            There are theories
                            of course   but
            how far back can a theory go

                    In the beginning—

a bird hits the window
    like a stone
in water   and the rings
     ripple outward

                    —earth was without form   and void
                but an X gave it shape
                            from darkness to (f)light
                So the word goes   his words

        Everyone likes a good story

            I can't tell one
                    bird from the next
                I know nuthatch from finch
        wren from siskin from waxwing
            but not one from its own kind

              Each is the other
                           as they gather
                                   herethengonethenhereagain
    one bird   leading to the next and the next
                            one   standing for the many

A city mortar-ripped
            the rings ripple outward
then everything happens at once—
              floodmudslidejihadelection—

and in fly X's
to drink from the eyes of the dead

            We forget and forget—
even snow surprises us
       even the cold
as if earth didn't turn
            unless we turned it

snow   snow snow snow
             Not a single flake alike
but all of them   spoken for
         and we think nothing of it

chickadee   nuthatch   jay
         Think bird is bird is bird is

         But if I push the edges out
something gives:
         the bird flies
    out of its name-cage

    and I can almost see
                              form   set free

Bird is what
    mind makes

        when the eye
        says flight

       bird is
       mind   made up

                        *

                        Mind is snow
                            falling out of the sky's
                  mouth   white
                         is the color
                                of a soul:

                                white

                                          is
                                winter's little   green
                                        truth

There in the thicket behind the bird feeders:
                those bushes
                          with their branches stripped of

              The bark red as wine
 Red   I tell you

          An X doesn't land in them
                Nothing happens
Just the branches   and the red

I breathe out
           for the trees
                breathe
  out
          for me

    A flock of snow flies up
             in a vortex of light
  and the eye says
               tiny white moths

      Yes: the invisible rides on the back
        of the visible   and this day
                    is struck with itself

Even the long aches of shadows shine out
                as they reach
    to be not shadow anymore   but tree:
                      tree tree   tree

  A bird on the feeder
         a world upside down:
                ɥɔʇɐɥʇnu

    Blink   and the bird
   never left
                      here then gone
                         then here again

     When I close my eyes
        the world   stands still

     I am the blink

    Why bird   is because
                  they're never not here
while I am always
        a glimpse behind

                              The project
                is an hourglass I turn
    over and over
watching time replace itself

                jaay   jaay jaaay
           riding on the back
         of the invisible

       I watch these birds from my cage
            Such clear glass
         I can almost believe
                       it is sky
   I'm looking through
            but the reflection from my lamp
     puts me in the air
               with them
and they fly alongside me
        as if   out of
                      pity

iii.

                  I'm at my desk
          Around me all of these books
so many stones
        feathers and nests   perched
                beneath windows I helped install
       So many windows

           Who was it made all this

Out there: the winter spiders
                     nestle under their bark
               larva   their rotting logs
          chelydra   their mud   What a vast
library mud is   What a holding that maple
 hollowed by lightning   and the subnivean zone
               a-mazed by voles
Every dark place another window
          into a new room

I flushed two grouse
                from under a spruce—
       three jump-started
                     hearts
                        wingbeat in snow:

  one foot
            the other
       tracks only   so deep

Dusk breaks over the mountain
                like a gate winging open
and I sense in the stillness
       something flown:

A cardinal   I said

  What I meant was
      red in winter is redder
        than green is green come spring

  I should have said
    look: there is a moment
calling you   calling us all

               *

              One goes where one is

      Sleep lost to me again
                              or was insomnia the dream

        Now dawn spreads across the frosted window
                                  and flares into the room

      I close my eyes and wake:
            three quick notes   and a pause

                            three quick notes—
                          say *titmouse*

          The light is a coverlet
          the way a pond is a field in winter

and under the ice under the snow
      the world's asleep   slowed

                    to the barest   pulse
                          What is the pause for

Nothing wants to be itself
                for long: winter loosens hold
drips off soffet   eave   branch
                      seeps into stone's creases
and the pond transluces—

        its language rising from its throat
in an upseep   a reverse kind of weeping
                      What is the Inuit word for ice
                that buckles under your weight
                        but doesn't break

And it is here I flushed a bird from the story
        of a pine
                  like a pale hand   a hand-
kerchief   crying as it flew—
                one note for every wingbeat
Dove I said

        What I meant was   *daughter*
you'll be alright   I meant
    child   come take my hand
I should have said   *break my heart*
I should have said   *world*

*

We forget and forget—
as if earth didn't turn
unless we

Saw a fox last night
            behind a snow-laden spruce
                      at the edge of a dream—
eye-to-eye we spoke
        without words
    No matter   what was said

This morning   a squirrel
            under the tray feeder
                    scrounges for drops—
tail-flick with every muscle-twitch
                      a kind of dream-speak

      Cold presses the day down
      and listening quiets the looking:

              tsee   tsee tseetsee
There   in the top of that spruce

                     so high-pitched
                     it's barely sound

Barely a bird   six grams at five below
           and somehow they're not dying

              kinglets   I said

          What I meant was   bird
                  is not bird is not bird

                I meant
           they're out here   everywhere

holding the world
    on their tiny backs

                *

            We come in and out
              of our cages
           sometimes to feed them

Acknowledgments

I am grateful to the editors of *The Massachusetts Review*, where this book's title poem first appeared. I am forever indebted to Jody Gladding, David Wojahn and Terry Johnson for their close, thoughtful readings, enduring support, and for their friendship. I would like to express my gratitude to contest judge, Natasha Kochicheril Moni, and the editors of *Concrete Wolf* for honoring this work with the award of publication. And, always, I thank you, Holly, Lily, and Tim, for your unconditional love and encouragement.

About the Author

Patty Crane's poems have appeared widely, including in *Bellevue Literary Review*, *The Massachusetts Review* and *West Branch*. Her translations of Swedish poet and Nobel laureate Tomas Tranströmer have appeared in *Blackbird*, *PEN Poetry Series*, and *New York Times Magazine*, among others, and are collected in her bi-lingual volume, *Bright Scythe* (Sarabande Books, 2015). Her awards include a MacDowell fellowship, Stanford Calderwood fellow, *Atlanta Review* International Prize, *Two Rivers Review* Poetry Prize, and two Pushcart nominations. She lives in a small hilltown in the Berkshires of western Massachusetts.

www.ingramcontent.com/pod-product-compliance
Lightning Source LLC
Chambersburg PA
CBHW060501010526
44118CB00018B/2500